# STAR WARS

## WORKBOOKS

# READING SKILLS

**FOR AGES 6–7**

BY THE EDITORS OF BRAIN QUEST
EDUCATIONAL CONSULTANT: CHARLOTTE RABY

D1335834

**SCHOLASTIC**

Scholastic Children's Books
Euston House,
24 Eversholt Street,
London NW1 1DB, UK

A division of Scholastic Ltd
London ~ New York ~ Toronto ~ Sydney ~ Auckland
Mexico City ~ New Delhi ~ Hong Kong

First published in the USA by Workman Publishing in 2014.
This edition published in the UK by Scholastic Ltd in 2016.
© & TM 2016 LUCASFILM LTD.

STAR WARS is a registered trademark of Lucasfilm Ltd.
BRAIN QUEST is a registered trademark of Workman Publishing Co., Inc., and Groupe Play Bac, S.A.

Workbook series design by Raquel Jaramillo
Cover illustration by Mike Sutfin
Interior illustrations by Scott Cohn

ISBN 978 1407 16295 9

Printed in Malaysia

2 4 6 8 10 9 7 5 3 1

Papers used by Scholastic Children's Books are made from woods grown in sustainable forests.

www.scholastic.co.uk

# STAR WARS

## WORKBOOKS

This workbook belongs to:

_____

# Jar Jar Words

A **grapheme** is a sound written down. There are many ways to write the 44 sounds in the English language.

Use the grapheme **ar** to complete the words. Now read the word aloud.

Jar Jar

 g___den

 p___ty

 MagnaGu___ds

 D___th Maul

 st___

 f___m

Write all the **ar** words in alphabetical order.

harm

dart

park

yard

art

large

march

cart

smart

start

far

_____

_____

_____

_____

_____

_____

_____

_____

_____

Write a sentence with one or more of the **ar** words on the list.

_____

_____

# Your Turn!

The sound 'ur' can be written in many different ways.

Read the words and circle the 'ur' sound.

How many different spellings of the 'ur' sound have you found?

herd

first

third

trooper

purple

purse

search

research

learn

birthday

survive

hurt

shirt

circle

perfect

burn

earth

bird

podracer

universe

Now sort the words into the boxes.

## ear

_____

_____

_____

_____

_____

_____

I found _____ ways to spell
the 'ear' sound.

## er

_____

_____

_____

_____

_____

_____

I found _____ ways to spell
the 'er' sound.

## ir

_____

_____

_____

_____

_____

_____

I found _____ ways to spell
the 'ir' sound.

## ur

_____

_____

_____

_____

_____

_____

I found _____ ways to spell
the 'ur' sound.

# Rancor Game

Read the words in the boxes. Use the clues to help you unscramble the words.

horns   more   soar   rancor   floor   orbit   four   roar

Jabba the Hutt has one of these in his palace.

C R O R N A   _ _ _ _ _ _

Saesee Tiin has these coming out of his head.

R H N S O   _ _ _ _ _

Planets do this around a sun.

B T O R I   _ _ _ _ _

The opposite of "less" is this word.

R E O M   _ _ _ _

Chewbacca often makes this sound.

O R A R   _ _ _ _

The opposite of "ceiling" is this.

O L O F R   _ _ _ _ _

This is another word for "fly".

R O A S   _ _ _ _

This number comes before "five".

U O R F   _ _ _ _

All of the words you unscrambled have the same vowel sound as **rancor**, but they are spelled differently.

Sort the words by how the '**or**' sound has been spelt into the correct boxes.

**or**
_____
_____

**oar**
_____
_____
_____

**oor**
_____
_____

**ore**
_____
_____

**our**
_____
_____

Find the words you have just sorted in the word search.

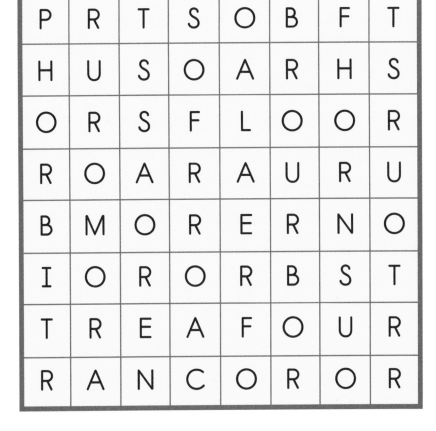

| P | R | T | S | O | B | F | T |
|---|---|---|---|---|---|---|---|
| H | U | S | O | A | R | H | S |
| O | R | S | F | L | O | O | R |
| R | O | A | R | A | U | R | U |
| B | M | O | R | E | R | N | O |
| I | O | R | O | R | B | S | T |
| T | R | E | A | F | O | U | R |
| R | A | N | C | O | R | O | R |

# Count Down!

Two common spellings of the '**ow**' sound are '**ou**' as in **count** and '**ow**' as in **down**.

Use '**ow**' or '**ou**' to complete the words in the crossword grid.

## ACROSS

**3.** There are 12 Jedi who sit on the Jedi High (C _ _ ncil).

**4.** Jar Jar Binks is clumsy. He falls (d _ _ n) a lot!

**5.** Coruscant is a city full of tall (t _ _ ers).

**6.** Boba Fett is a (b _ _ nty) hunter.

**9.** (C _ _ nt) Dooku is also known as Darth Tyranus.

**11.** Amidala is a queen but she doesn't wear a (cr _ _ n).

## DOWN

**1.** The opposite of "whisper" is (sh _ _ t).

**2.** The Force is a (p _ _ erful) energy field.

**6.** Wookiees have (br _ _ n) fur.

**7.** You use a (t _ _ el) to dry yourself.

**8.** The past tense of "find" is (f _ _ nd).

**10.** Mos Espa is a (t _ _ n) on Tatooine.

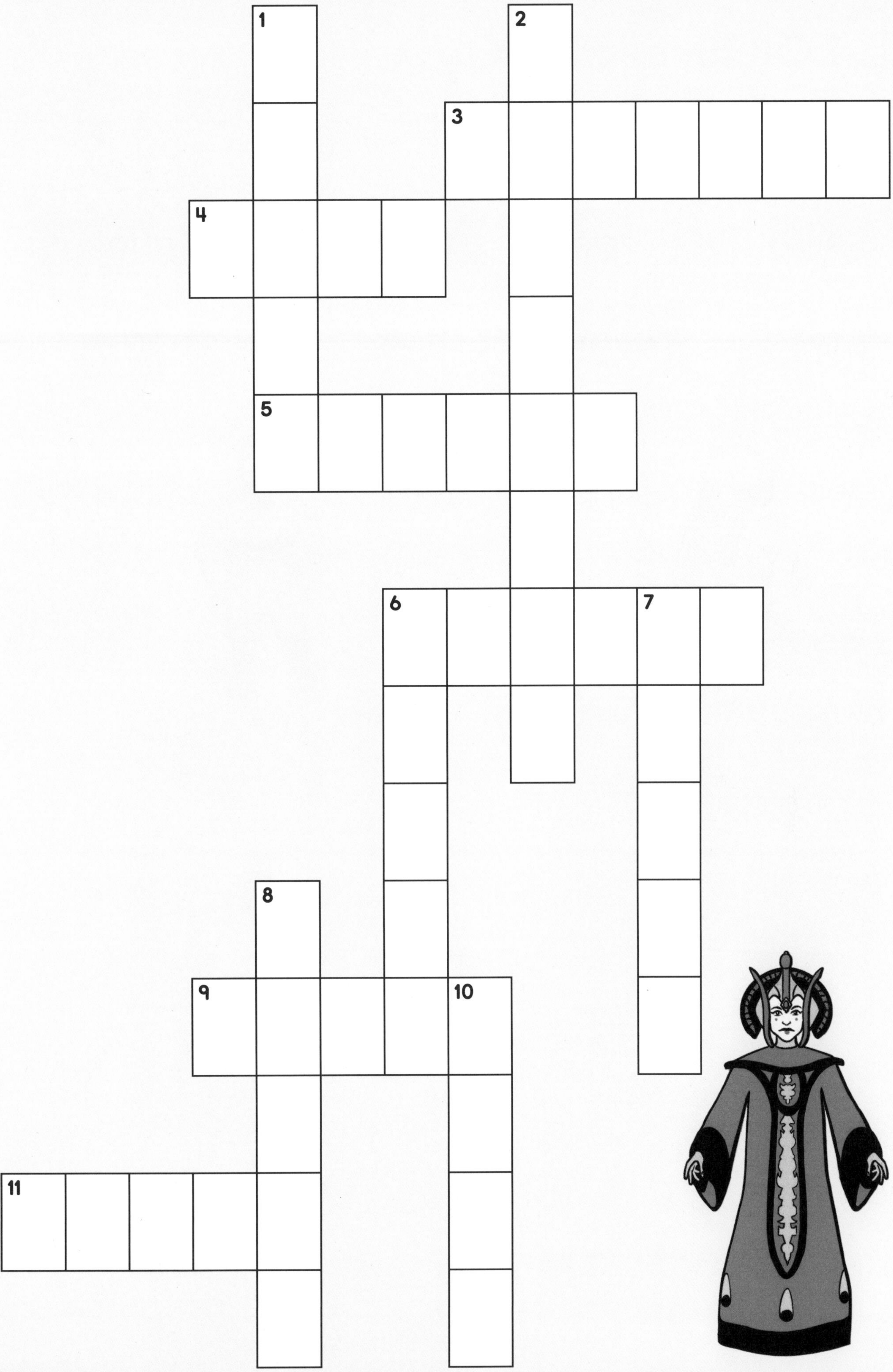
1
2
3
4
5
6
7
8
9
10
11

# Droids Destroy!

Sort the words by spelling pattern into the boxes below.

droid    boy    point    annoy    toy    choice

voice    royal    destroy    enjoy    boil

join    oil

**oi**

_____

_____

_____

_____

_____

_____

**oy**

_____

_____

_____

_____

_____

# Look at the Moon!

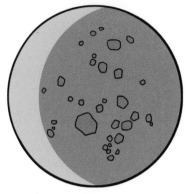

The grapheme '**oo**' can make two sounds.

It can make the short vowel sound in words such as **book** and **look.**

It can make a long vowel sound such as **moon** and **swoop.**

Sort the words by their '**oo**' sound into the boxes below.

spoon   tooth   cook   hook   shook   wood

loose   Dooku   balloon   hood   took

Naboo   book   good   soon   Plo Koon

## look

_____   _____   _____

_____   _____   _____

_____   _____   _____

## moon

_____   _____   _____

_____   _____   _____

# Opposites!

**Antonyms** are words that have opposite meanings.

Read each sentence. Circle the **antonym** of the underlined word in each sentence.

Jango Fett can fly <u>up</u> in the air with his jetpack.

around     down     high

Anakin's podracer is <u>first</u> in the race!

last     second     next

It is so sunny and <u>hot</u> on Tatooine!

warm     bright     cold

Chewbacca is very <u>tall</u>.

furry     short     happy

Mace Windu is a very <u>wise</u> Jedi Master.

silly     tough     sad

Han Solo says that the *Millennium Falcon* is a <u>fast</u> ship.

speedy     slow     tired

Write a sentence for each of the **antonyms**.

_____

_____

_____

_____

_____

_____

_____

_____

_____

# Similar!

**Synonyms** are words that have similar meanings.

Read each sentence. Circle the **synonym** of the underlined word in each sentence.

Yoda may be the smallest Jedi, but he is also the most <u>powerful</u>.

happy    weak    strong

C-3PO can <u>speak</u> over six million languages.

silent    talk    sing

R2-D2 is <u>tiny</u> compared to C-3PO.

big    same    little

Padmé is <u>brave</u> when she battles the nexu.

fearless    scared    sleepy

Many Imperial officers are <u>scared</u> of Darth Vader.

unafraid    frightened    loyal

Chewbacca is Han Solo's <u>best</u> friend.

enemy    only    greatest

Write a sentence for each of the **synonyms**.

_____

_____

_____

_____

_____

_____

_____

_____

_____

# Night, Knight!

**Homophones** are words that sound the same but have different spellings and meanings.

Read each sentence. Circle the correct **homophone**.

Luke is a Jedi (Knight) / **Night**.

The **some** / **sum** of three plus three is six.

Tatooine has two **suns** / **sons**.

Princess Leia is on a **peace** / **piece** mission.

No one **guessed** / **guest** that Luke was Leia's brother!

Rancors eat a lot of **meet** / **meat**.

It would **be** / **bee** amazing to fly with a jet pack.

Write a sentence for each **homophone** that you did not circle.

_____

_____

_____

_____

_____

_____

_____

_____

_____

_____

_____

# Batches of Lightsabers!

**Plural** means more than one. For most words, add **s** to make a singular noun plural. For words ending in **sh**, **ch**, **tch**, **s** or **x**, add **es**.

Write the plural for each word by adding **s** or **es**.

lightsaber_____          batch_____

tree_____                box_____

glass_____               bench_____

bush_____                bus_____

Ewok_____                watch_____

stormtrooper_____        ax_____

# Weird Plurals!

Some singular nouns do not take **s** or **es** to form plurals. These nouns have **irregular plurals**. An irregular plural changes the spelling of the word.

Draw a line from the noun to its **irregular plural**.

| | |
|---|---|
| tooth | mice |
| child | teeth |
| goose | men |
| foot | feet |
| woman | geese |
| man | people |
| mouse | children |
| person | oxen |
| ox | women |

Write each of the **irregular plurals** on the lines below.

_____   _____   _____

_____   _____   _____

_____   _____   _____

# Tell Me Something!

A **complete sentence** has a subject and a verb. The subject of the **sentence** is either a noun or a pronoun. A noun stands for a person, place or thing. A verb represents the action in a sentence.

A **phrase** is a group of words that makes sense but does not include a verb.

Is it a **sentence** or a **phrase**? Underline the verbs to identify the sentences.

Tusken Raiders <u>live</u> in tents.

The stars in the galaxy.

Luke, Leia and Han.

Chewbacca can fly the *Millennium Falcon.*

The small, furry Ewok.

C-3PO is very shiny.

Darth Vader wears a mask.

The droids you're looking for.

It happened a long time ago.

Change the **phrases** into **sentences**. Make sure you use a verb.

_____

_____

_____

_____

_____

_____

_____

_____

_____

_____

_____

_____

# Statement or Question?

A **question** is a sentence that asks something.

A **statement** is a sentence that tells what someone or something is doing, or what someone or something is.

A **question mark** tells us the sentence is a question.

Copy each sentence on the line below it. Add a **full stop** if the sentence is a **statement** or a **question mark** if the sentence is a **question**.

How many Ewoks do you see

_____

Will Anakin become a Jedi Knight

_____

He wears a black robe

_____

Who is looking for Obi-Wan Kenobi

_____

Will Lando help Han escape

_____

Padmé loves Anakin

_____

# Exclamations and Commands!

An **exclamation** is a sentence that shows a strong feeling.

A **command** is a sentence that tells someone to do something.

An **exclamation mark** tells us that the sentence is a command or an exclamation.

Decide if each sentence is a **question**, **exclamation** or **command**. Copy the sentence using the correct punctuation.

Do we need to get out of this asteroid field.

_____

Watch out.

_____

I thought you said this ship was fast.

_____

Can we go any faster.

_____

That asteroid is coming right at us.

_____

We did it.

_____

# Spelling Break!

Write each of these words two times.

universe _____ _____

purpose _____ _____

choice _____ _____

clumsy _____ _____

glass _____ _____

orbit _____ _____

watches _____ _____

learn _____ _____

floor _____ _____

royal _____ _____

captain _____ _____

circle _____ _____

axes _____ _____

asteroid _____ _____

knife _____ _____

found _____ _____

Choose any six of the words. Write a sentence for each one.

_____

_____

_____

_____

_____

_____

_____

_____

_____

# Common or Proper?

A **common noun** is a word or group of words that stands for a person, place, thing or idea.

A **proper noun** is a word or group of words that names a specific person, place, thing or idea. A proper noun starts with a capital letter.

Underline the **common nouns** in each sentence.
Draw a circle around the **proper nouns**.

 Anakin uses many different tools to build the droid.

Queen Amidala comes from Naboo.

Both the Jedi and the Sith use lightsabers.

The moons orbit around the planets because of gravity.

Many strange creatures live in the swamps of Dagobah.

Sort all the **nouns** you underlined and circled in the boxes below.
Don't forget to capitalise the proper nouns.

| **person** | **place** | **thing** | **ideas** |
|---|---|---|---|
| ___ | ___ | ___ | ___ |
| ___ | ___ | ___ | ___ |
| ___ | ___ | ___ | ___ |
| ___ | ___ | ___ | ___ |
| ___ | ___ | ___ | ___ |

# Pronouns!

A **pronoun** is a word that can take the place of a noun. Read the **pronouns** in the boxes.

Rewrite each sentence with a **pronoun** in place of the underlined word or words.

| He | She | it | We | They |

<u>Kit Fisto and Plo Koon</u> fight the droids.

<u>They fight the droids.</u>

<u>Aayla</u> joins the battle.

_____

<u>Mace Windu</u> comes to help.

_____

Mace says, "<u>All of us</u> are stronger than they are!"

_____

_____

He quickly destroys <u>a droid</u> with his lightsaber.

_____

_____

# Younglings!

The **subject** is the do-er or be-er in a sentence. Usually you find the subject before the verb.

The **subject** is a word or group of words that tells us who or what the sentence is about. The subject can be a **noun** or **pronoun**.

Underline the **subject**. Circle the **noun** in the subject.

The Jedi Temple is an exciting place.

Younglings from every part of the galaxy
become Jedi Knights.

Yoda teaches the younglings every day.

The tallest youngling is called Gungi.

Gungi is a Wookiee.

All the younglings train and play together.

If they train hard, they may grow up to be
Jedi Masters like Yoda!

# Adjectives

An **adjective** gives more information about a noun. Colour, size and number words can be **adjectives**.

Circle the **noun**. Underline the **adjective** or **adjectives**.

furry (Wookiee)

blue lightsaber

green skin

five brave younglings

big rock

two eyes

# Jedi Knights!

A **verb** represents the action in a sentence. It tells us what someone or something does. Verbs in the present tense tell us what is happening now.

Use the **verbs** to say what the Jedi Knights are doing.

mends    talks    jumps

walks    picks    climbs

Kit Fisto _____ a bantha down the road.

Aayla Secura _____ a flower.

Plo Koon _____ to Bultar Swan about the weather.

Saesee Tiin _____ the droid with his tools.

Luminara Unduli _____ over the puddle.

Shaak Ti _____ up a tower.

**Verbs in the past tense** tell us what has happened. You add the suffix **ed** to make many verbs into the **past tense**.

A **suffix** is added to the end of a word to change its meaning or verb tense.

Rewrite each sentence in the past tense by changing the verb. Replace the **s** or **es** with **ed**.

Kit Fisto walked a bantha down the road.

# The Battle of Geonosis!

Adverbs give us more information about verbs. Adverbs can tell us where, when or how something happens.

Underline the verb in each sentence. Circle the adverb.

Mace Windu and 200 Jedi travelled (quickly) to Geonosis.

They battled the droids there.

The Jedi bravely fought the enemy droids.

Later, Yoda arrived with thousands of clone troopers.

The Jedi and clone troopers surrounded the droids inside the arena.

Afterwards, the Jedi left the planet.

Write each **adverb** you circled in the correct box below.

where?

_____

_____

when?

_____

_____

how?

_____

_____

Write a sentence for three of the **adverbs**.

_____

_____

_____

_____

_____

# A Poem

Read the **poem**. Then answer the questions.

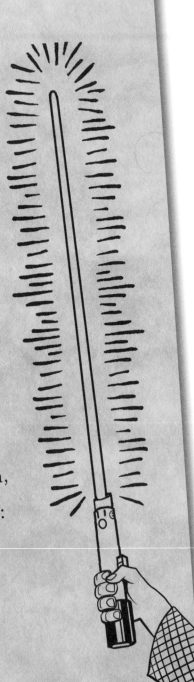

## The Lightsaber

When in the darkest time of night
Impossible can seem the light,
The memory of every sun
Fading, one by one by one.

So easy to forget that hope
Can be the strongest kind of rope
To pull us back upon the course:
And find a way back to the Force.

In Ilum's icy caves of gloom,
Crystals shine like flowers bloom,
The light in them will never fade:
The source of my Jedi blade.

"The Lightsaber" is a **poem** that **rhymes**.

Fill in the boxes with **rhyming words** from the poem. Then add your own **rhyming word** to each of the lists.

sun

_____

_____

night

_____

_____

hope

_____

_____

gloom

_____

_____

course

_____

_____

fade

_____

_____

Answer the questions about the **poem** "The Lightsaber".

The first line of the poem sets the mood:
"When in the darkest time of night..." Which
word best describes the mood of the poem?

☐ happy     ☐ thoughtful     ☐ silly

The author of the poem compares "hope" to:

☐ a strong rope     ☐ an icy cave     ☐ a crystal

The author compares crystals to flowers: "Crystals shine
like flowers bloom." What do you think the author meant
by this comparison?

_____

_____

From whose point of view is the poem written?
The last line of the poem is a clue.

_____

_____

Use your rhyming words from page 37 to write a poem. It can be any length. It can be about anything.

_____

_____

_____

_____

_____

_____

_____

_____

_____

_____

# A Fable

Read the **fable**. Answer the questions about each part of the story.

## The Ewoks and the Duloks

Once upon a time on the forest moon of Endor, a big storm began to brew in the mountains. The Ewoks, seeing the dark clouds above the mountains, prepared for the storm. They threw ropes around the oldest trees to brace them against the wind. They dug shelters underground, which they covered with wax to make them waterproof. They gathered as many nuts and berries as they could find, and stored them away inside the shelters.

The Duloks, seeing their cousins toiling so hard, were scornful.

"Why are you all working so much?" they asked.

"There is a big storm brewing in the mountains!" answered the Ewoks. "The storm is heading towards us. We are making sure we have enough to eat in case the storm lasts a long time."

• 1 •

The Duloks looked up. The sky was clear and blue, and the sun shone brightly. The passing breeze was gentle. The air smelled of almonds and lavender.

"What storm?" the Duloks replied scornfully. "It is a beautiful day! And there is plenty to eat! Why worry about storms that may come tomorrow when today is so bright and lovely?"

The Ewoks shrugged and kept on working.

The Duloks laughed.

"What silly Ewoks you are!" they said, and went off to play.

• 2 •

## Where is the story set?

_____

_____

## How would you describe the Ewoks?
(Tick as many boxes as you want)

☐ hardworking   ☐ rude   ☐ nice
☐ clever   ☐ lazy   ☐ mean

## How would you describe the Duloks?
(Tick as many boxes as you want)

☐ hardworking   ☐ rude   ☐ nice
☐ clever   ☐ lazy   ☐ mean

How do the Ewoks know that a storm is coming?

_____

_____

Name one thing the Ewoks did to prepare for the storm.

_____

_____

What did the Duloks do while the Ewoks prepared for the storm?

_____

The next day, the storm reached the forest. The sky darkened. The wind whipped the trees. The rain poured.

In the part of the forest where the Ewoks lived, the trees that they had lashed with ropes withstood the wind. The Ewoks stayed cosy and dry deep within their shelters. Although the storm lasted several days, they had plenty of food to eat.

In the part of the forest where the Duloks lived, the trees began to fall. Their tree huts were destroyed.

The Duloks had nowhere to hide from the storm. They ran to where the Ewoks lived.

"Please, help us!" they pleaded.

The Ewoks, seeing their cousins in such distress, opened up their shelters and let them in. They shared their nuts and berries with them.

After the storm ended, the Ewoks and the Duloks left the shelters. They looked at all the damage the storm had done.

"Thank you," said the Duloks. "It was kind of you to take us in."

"When hard times hit one of us," answered the Ewoks, "they hit us all."

**The End**

What happened to the Duloks when the storm came?

_____

What did the Ewoks do when the Duloks went to them for help?

☐ They laughed at the Duloks.

☐ They gave them shelter.

What lesson do you think the fable teaches?

_____

_____

# Spelling Break!

Write each of these words two times.

people

_____  _____

planet

_____  _____

source

_____  _____

bright

_____  _____

creatures

_____  _____

gravity

_____  _____

exciting

_____  _____

never

_____  _____

laugh

_____  _____

shelter

_____  _____

course

_____  _____

impossible

_____  _____

destroy

_____  _____

brew

_____  _____

poem

_____  _____

white

_____  _____

Choose any six of the words. Write a sentence for each one.

_____

_____

_____

_____

_____

_____

_____

_____

_____

# An Action Story

Read the **action story**. Then answer the questions.

The Podrace

On Tatooine, podracing is a very popular sport. Fans come from all over the galaxy to watch. Podracing is also a very dangerous sport. Podracers have big engines. They fly very fast. Sometimes they crash during the race.

Anakin Skywalker is a gifted podracer. Although he is only a boy, he is one of the best racers on the planet. He has very quick reflexes. He builds his own podracers! But Anakin's mother, Shmi, does not like Anakin to race. She is afraid he will get hurt.

· 1 ·

Anakin and Shmi live in a hut that is owned by Watto. They work for him. They are not allowed to work for anyone else.

One day, Qui-Gon Jinn makes a deal with Watto. If Anakin wins the podrace, Watto will let Anakin go free. So Anakin enters the race. Padmé Amidala is worried that Anakin will hurt himself, but Qui-Gon Jinn believes that Anakin is the Chosen One. He believes the Force will help Anakin to win.

The race is about to begin. The stadium is full of fans. No one except for Qui-Gon Jinn, Shmi and Padmé think that Anakin can win the podrace. Everyone knows that one of the podracers, a Dug named Sebulba, is a cheat. He will stop at nothing to win.

Ready? Steady? Go! Zoom! The podracers start the race. They fly across the desert. All except for Anakin! He has trouble getting his engines to start.

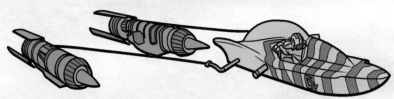

After a few minutes, Anakin starts his engines. He catches up to the other podracers by the time they get to the Canyon Dune Turn. Here they have to be careful: Tusken Raiders fire blasters at them!

• 2 •

When the podracers fly across a desert called Bindy Bend, Anakin gets hit by another podracer. For a few seconds, it looks as if his engine will fall apart – but he fixes it. By the time the podracers emerge onto the Hutt Flats, the last leg of the race, Anakin is in second place. Sebulba is in first place!

The two of them fly neck and neck across the desert. Sebulba slams his podracer into Anakin's a few times, and Anakin can't turn one of his engines back on. It looks as if Anakin will lose the race.

But wait – Anakin has an idea. He attaches his podracer to Sebulba's! When Sebulba tries to pull away, his podracer breaks apart. Sebulba crashes.

Anakin wins the race – and his freedom!

## The End

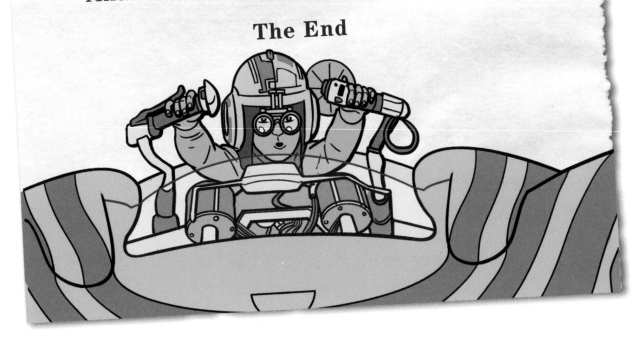

Answer the questions about the **action story** "The Podrace".

On which planet is podracing a very popular sport?

_____

Give one reason why podracing is a dangerous sport.

_____

Who is Shmi?

_____

Name all of the characters in the story.

_____

_____

_____

Why does Qui-Gon Jinn think that Anakin will win?

_____

_____

_____

What happens to the podracers in the Canyon Dune Turn?

_____

Number the pictures from 1 to 4 to show what happened first, second, third and fourth.

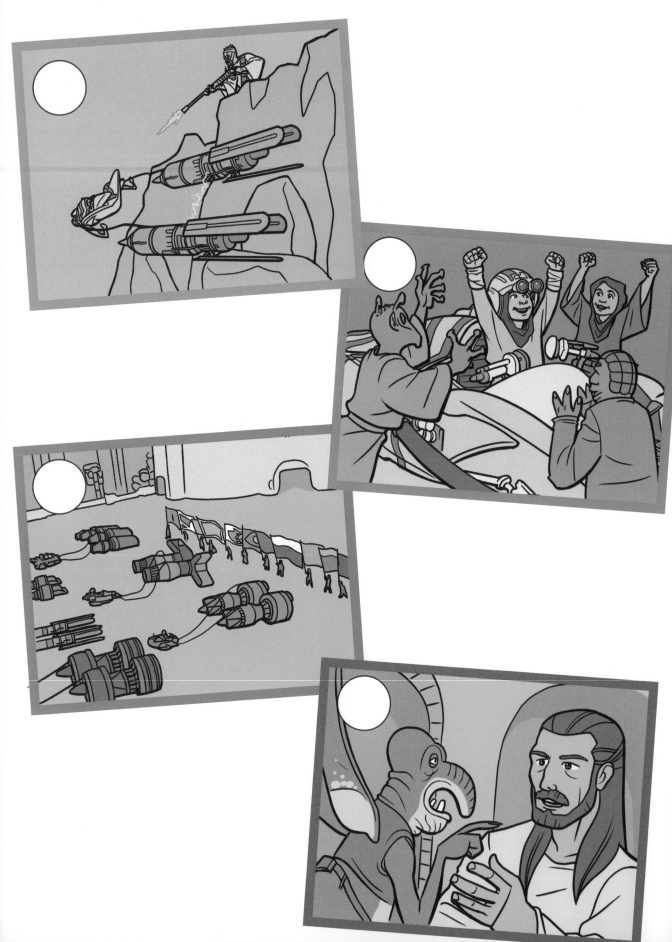

# A Play

Read the **play** out loud by yourself or with friends.
Then answer the questions.

The Saga of
Anakin Skywalker

JEDI STORYTELLER: The story of Anakin Skywalker is one of the most famous stories in the galaxy. It begins a long time ago, on the desert planet Tatooine, where the boy named Anakin Skywalker lived with his mother. The Force was very strong with young Anakin.

One day, Padmé Amidala landed on Tatooine. Padmé was a few years older than Anakin. She was a queen, but she did not wear a crown. When Anakin first saw her, he thought she was the most beautiful person he'd ever seen in his life.

ANAKIN: Are you an angel?

PADMÉ: What?

-1-

ANAKIN: An angel. I've heard the deep space pilots talk about them. They are the most beautiful creatures in the universe. They live on the Moons of Iego, I think.

PADMÉ: I've never heard of angels.

ANAKIN: You must be one . . . maybe you just don't know it.

JEDI STORYTELLER: Many years later, Padmé and Anakin met again. Anakin was no longer a little boy. He had grown up. He was a brave Jedi Padawan. A Padawan is an apprentice or a student. When Padmé's life was in danger, Anakin protected her.

Shortly afterwards, they were both captured. They were taken to the Geonosian Battle Arena, where they fought fierce creatures. Padmé battled the nexu. Anakin battled the reek. They both escaped. In time, Padmé and Anakin fell in love and married.

-2-

JEDI STORYTELLER: Over time, Anakin turned to the dark side of the Force. Padmé did not like this. Nor did Obi-Wan Kenobi, Anakin's former teacher. He and Anakin had a lightsaber duel on the lava planet, Mustafar.

OBI-WAN: You have allowed this Dark Lord to twist your mind until now . . . you have become the very thing you swore to destroy.

ANAKIN: Don't lecture me, Obi-Wan. I see through the lies of the Jedi. I do not fear the dark side as you do. I have brought peace, justice, freedom and security to my new Empire.

JEDI STORYTELLER: Anakin lost the lightsaber duel. Obi-Wan left him on Mustafar, but Darth Sidious rescued Anakin. Darth Sidious turned Anakin into his apprentice . . . Darth Vader.

-3-

Plot the **play** "The Saga of Anakin Skywalker".

Explain what happens in the beginning, middle and end of the play.

## Beginning

Explain about when Anakin was a little boy.

_____

_____

_____

## Middle

Explain about when Padmé and Anakin were taken to the Geonosian Battle Arena.

_____

_____

_____

## End

Explain about when Anakin turned to the dark side of the Force.

_____

_____

_____

_____

# A Short Story

Read the **short story** about Boba Fett. Then answer the questions.

## THE RISE OF BOBA FETT

**B**OBA FETT IS A LEGENDARY BOUNTY HUNTER. He can track down anybody – for a price. There is no corner of the galaxy, no space station, no remote planet in the Outer Rim, where Boba Fett won't go to find his prey.

But how did Boba Fett become a bounty hunter? It all started when he was a little boy. Boba Fett's father was the legendary Jango Fett, who had been raised by a fierce tribe of warriors known as the Mandalorians. Jango was such a supreme warrior, he was chosen to be the model for the clone trooper army. Boba was the very first clone created – an exact copy of his father. But Jango did not want Boba to be raised like the other clone troopers. Jango decided to raise him as his son. This is why Boba Fett has his own unique identity and personality.

1

Jango Fett trained Boba Fett to become a warrior. He taught him combat skills. He showed him how to use his armour, and how to fly his starfighter, the *Slave I*. When Jango died, Boba was forced to fend for himself. He relied on all the things his father had taught him to survive. Boba used his skills to become a bounty hunter.

**2**

A **cause** tells us why something happens. An **effect** is what happens. Draw a line to match each cause and effect in the short story "The Rise of Boba Fett".

# Cause

| Jango Fett was a supreme warrior. |

| Jango raised Boba as his son. |

| Jango died. |

# Effect

| Boba was forced to fend for himself. |

| Jango was chosen to become the model for the clone trooper army. |

| Boba has his own unique identity and personality. |

# Jedi Stories

Read the **stories** about the Jedi. Then answer the questions.

**Ki-Adi-Mundi** was a member of the Jedi Council. He was born on the planet Cerea. When he was four years old, he became a Padawan, an apprentice, to Master Yoda. He was a very powerful Jedi, and could move objects with his mind.

Ki-Adi-Mundi was exceptionally brave, and carried a blue-bladed lightsaber. Sadly, his clone troopers turned on him on Mygeeto, after Order 66 was activated.

**Plo Koon** came from the planet Dorin. He wore protective goggles and a mask because he could not breathe the oxygen found on most planets. He was a member of the Jedi Council.

When Plo Koon was a Padawan, his Jedi Master was a Wookiee named Tyvokka. In time, Plo Koon took on his own Padawan, who was named Bultar Swan.

Plo Koon's lightsaber was blue. Although he was a very skilled pilot, he died when clone troopers fired on his starfighter in Cato Neimoidia. He was another victim of Order 66.

**Kit Fisto** was a Nautolan from the planet Glee Anselm. Nautolans live in air or underwater. Nautolans are very good swimmers because their tendrils flare out like octopus tentacles underwater.

Kit Fisto had a green-bladed lightsaber. He was a very brave Jedi. His speciality was his ability to detect what his opponent was going to do next in battle. Unfortunately, Count Dooku proved to be too strong an opponent for Kit Fisto.

**Shaak Ti** was a Togrutan from the planet Shili. The hollow horns on top of her head gave her the power to "hear" things that other people could not hear. This gave her an edge in battle – especially battles involving large groups.

Shaak Ti fought bravely in the Battle of Geonosis with her blue-bladed lightsaber.

**Aayla Secura** was a Twi'lek from the planet Ryloth. Known for her intelligence and kindness, Aayla did not like to fight. She was more of a peacemaker, only using her blue-bladed lightsaber to defend herself. Aayla was a master of Force cloaking: the ability to become so still that other people cannot detect you.

Aayla was another victim of Order 66, when the clone troopers she was leading into battle on the planet Felucia turned against her.

**Order 66** was the command given that called for the immediate execution of the Jedi. The clone troopers were programmed to follow it without question or hesitation. The only person who could issue the command was Supreme Chancellor Palpatine. This was before everyone knew that he was also the Sith Lord, Darth Sidious.

Who is who? Write the name of the character on the line next to each picture.

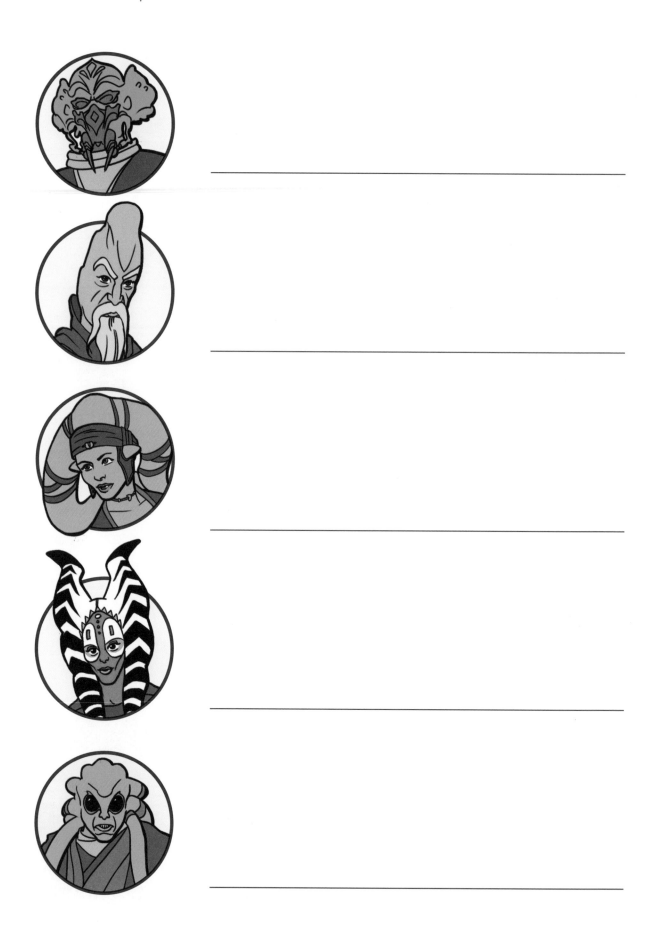

There were many details in each story.
Answer the questions about the Jedi stories.

Which Jedi did not have a blue lightsaber?

_____

When Ki-Adi-Mundi was a Padawan, who was his Jedi Master?

_____

Who was responsible for issuing Order 66?

_____

_____

Which Jedi was a Twi'lek?

_____

Circle the part of Kit Fisto's body
that helps him be a good swimmer.

All of the Jedi had special abilities. Write about two of them.

_____

_____

_____

_____

_____

_____

_____

What was Order 66?

_____

_____

_____

# A Biography

Read the **biography** of George Lucas. Then answer the questions.

# George Lucas
### Biography of a Filmmaker

Geor008 Walton Lucas, the creator of *Star Wars*, was born in Modesto, California, on May 14th, 1944. When he was growing up, he loved comic books. Some of his early favourites were the Flash Gordon comics, which were a series of science fiction adventure stories set in outer space.

Lucas also loved cars and motor racing. He dreamed of becoming a professional racing-car driver when he grew up. He started racing cars when he was a teenager. However, shortly before he left school, he had a serious car accident. This accident caused him to rethink becoming a professional racing-car driver.

Instead of racing cars, Lucas chose to study filmmaking at the University of Southern California. He made many student films. One of them, *THX 1138 4EB*, was a short film that received many student film awards.

Several years later, in 1971, Lucas founded his own film company, Lucasfilm. The second film Lucas made through Lucasfilm was called *American Graffiti*. The film was inspired by Lucas's high school experiences. It was a huge hit, and was nominated for five Academy Awards.

After the release of *American Graffiti*, Lucas decided he wanted to make a space fantasy film. He wanted it to be an adventure story set in outer space, like the Flash Gordon comics he loved so much as a child. In the early drafts of the film script, the story was called *The Star Wars*. By the time it came out on May 25th, 1977, it was called *Star Wars*.

*Star Wars* quickly became the most popular film ever made. Luke Skywalker, Princess Leia and Darth Vader became familiar characters all over the world. People started quoting lines from the film, such as: "May the Force be with you," and "Help me, Obi-Wan Kenobi. You're my only hope." Children wanted to play with *Star Wars* toys and games.

2

Lucas during the filming of *Attack of the Clones* in Tunisia

George Lucas had created a true pop culture phenomenon. In time, he made many other successful films, including *The Empire Strikes Back* and *Return of the Jedi*. More than fifteen years later, he made three more *Star Wars* films: *The Phantom Menace*, *Attack of the Clones* and *Revenge of the Sith*. He retired from Lucasfilm in 2012, and sold his company to Disney.

It's a good thing George Lucas decided not to become a racing-car driver. If he had, the world might never have had *Star Wars*!

3

Answer the questions about the biography of George Lucas.
Circle the correct answers.

## What is the main subject of the biography?

a) The creation of Lucasfilm.

b) Where George Lucas was born.

c) Racing-car driving.

d) How George Lucas became a filmmaker and made *Star Wars.*

## Based on the biography, why did George Lucas decide to study filmmaking?

a) He went to the University of Southern California.

b) A racing-car accident made him decide not to become a racing-car driver.

c) He had always loved films.

d) He founded Lucasfilm.

## What was the name of the film that came out in 1977?

a) *American Graffiti*

b) *Star Wars*

c) *THX 1138 4EB*

d) *Flash Gordon*

## What happened when *Star Wars* came out?

a) It became the most popular film of all time.

b) George Lucas decided to retire.

c) George Lucas created *American Graffiti*.

d) George Lucas founded Lucasfilm.

Circle the best word to complete each sentence.

George Lucas _____ cars and motor racing.

disliked    loved    liked

*American Graffiti* was _____ by George Lucas's high-school experience.

made    loved    inspired

George Lucas wanted to make an _____ story set in outer space.

exciting    adventure    upsetting

After *Star Wars* came out, Darth Vader became a _____ character to people around the world.

familiar    hated    beloved

Based on the text, why is it a good thing that George Lucas did not become a racing-car driver?

_____

_____

# Spelling Break!

Write each of these words two times.

popular

first

beautiful

student

clone

race

danger

duel

armour

chosen

famous

bounty

supreme

vines

driver

_____  _____

_____  _____

_____  _____

_____  _____

_____  _____

_____  _____

_____  _____

_____  _____

_____  _____

_____  _____

_____  _____

_____  _____

_____  _____

_____  _____

_____  _____

Choose any six of the words. Write a sentence for each one.

_____

_____

_____

_____

_____

_____

_____

_____

# A Letter to George Lucas

Here is a fan letter to George Lucas. The parts of the letter have been labelled, but there are some grammatical mistakes. Use the proofreading marks below to edit the mistakes.

| Proofreading Marks | | |
|---|---|---|
| ∧ Add text | ⊙ Add a full stop | ↑ Add a question mark |
| ≡ Capitalize letter | ℒ Take out | ◯ Spelling error |

Mr George Lucas  ←Heading

Lucasfilm

1110 Gorgas Avenue

San Francisco, CA 94129

Body

Dear Mr Lucas, ←Greeting

I love your movies! I like all six of them, but my favourite is Attack of the Clones. It was cool how padmé, Obi-Wan and anakin fort the arena creatures. I alsew liked how the clone tropers helped the Jedi. i have a pet mouse.

I heard you are making three new movies. Will those be about Luke Skywalker. I can't wait to see them.

Yours Sincerely, ←Closing

Cary (age 10) ← Signature

# A Letter From You

Would you like to write a letter to George Lucas?

Write a first draft of it here.

_____

_____

_____

_____

_____

_____

_____

_____

_____

Now proofread your letter to make sure you haven't made any mistakes.

Use this checklist to make sure!

☐ Are all the words spelled correctly?

☐ Does every sentence begin with a capital letter?

☐ Does every sentence end with a full stop or a question mark?

☐ Are names capitalised?

☐ Do you have a heading, greeting, body, closing and signature?

# An Article

Read the newspaper **article**. Then answer the questions.

May 26, 1977

# In a Galaxy Far, Far Away. . .

A review of a new movie called *Star Wars*

by *K. Lypen*

**LOS ANGELES, CALIFORNIA–**
Yesterday, *Star Wars: A New Hope* opened in cinemas across the country. Written and directed by George Lucas, this science-fiction movie is a fun and exciting adventure through outer space.

The plot revolves around Luke Skywalker, a young man living on a remote desert planet. Luke craves adventure. He wants to become a Jedi Knight, as his father had been. When a couple of droids land on his planet, he doesn't realise that his quest for adventure is about to come true.

The droids lead Luke to Obi-Wan Kenobi, a wise old hermit living in the desert. Obi-Wan, it turns out, is a Jedi Knight himself. He starts to train Luke Skywalker in the ways of the Force.

The Force is an energy field that lives inside and around all living things. Its powers can be used for good – or evil.

Together with the two droids, a cheeky pilot named Han Solo and a furry creature named Chewbacca, Luke and Obi-Wan set out to rescue Princess Leia. Leia is part of the Rebel Alliance that is working to defeat the evil Empire. She's been taken prisoner by Darth Vader. Vader was once a pupil of Obi-Wan Kenobi, who had trained him to become a Jedi Knight. That was before Vader turned to the dark side of the Force. Now Vader uses his Force powers for evil on behalf of the Empire.

Will the Rebel Alliance defeat the Empire? Will Luke become a Jedi Knight? This movie is destined to become a classic. It is a thrilling adventure story that everyone in the family will love. Two thumbs up!

The sentences below are all highlighted in the article.

Put a cross by the meaning that fits the underlined word in each sentence.

Luke <u>craves</u> adventure.

☐ wants  ☐ hates

The droids lead Luke to Obi-Wan Kenobi, a <u>wise</u> old hermit living in the desert.

☐ thoughtful  ☐ friend

Vader was once a <u>pupil</u> of Obi-Wan Kenobi, who had trained him to become a Jedi Knight.

☐ teacher  ☐ student

Now Vader uses his Force powers for evil <u>on behalf of</u> the Empire.

☐ on half of  ☐ on the side of

Will the Rebel Alliance <u>defeat</u> the Empire?

☐ beat  ☐ lose to

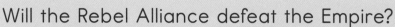

Draw a line from the vocabulary words used in the article (in the blue boxes) to the words that mean the same thing (in the yellow boxes).

plot

remote

quest

evil

thrilling

distant, hard to get to

exciting, fun

storyline

a search for, hunt

bad

Write a sentence for each of the words.

_____

_____

_____

_____

# All About Lightsabers!

Read the **essay** about lightsabers. Then answer the questions.

# LIGHTSABERS

The favourite weapon of both the Jedi and the Sith, lightsabers are extremely powerful – but only in the hands of those who know how to use them! With blades made of pure energy, they can cut through anything (except another lightsaber).

Most Jedi have blue- or green-bladed lightsabers.* Jedi construct their own lightsabers from crystals they collect on Ilum, a mountainous ice planet. The lightsaber hilt is a complicated piece of machinery (see chart to the right). Every Jedi designs his or her own lightsaber to suit his or her needs.

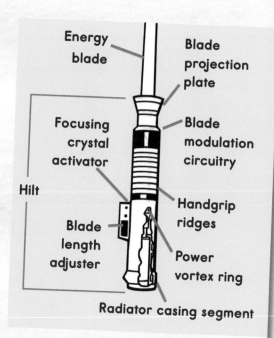

Energy blade

Blade projection plate

Focusing crystal activator

Blade modulation circuitry

Hilt

Handgrip ridges

Blade length adjuster

Power vortex ring

Radiator casing segment

The Sith also make their own lightsabers. They are always red because they use the dark side of the Force.

* Footnote: Mace Windu's lightsaber is an exception to this. His lightsaber is purple because of his unique connection with the Force.

Answer the questions about the essay on lightsabers.

What is the main purpose of this essay?

_____

_____

_____

_____

What colour lightsabers do the Sith have? Why?

_____

_____

What is the only thing that lightsabers cannot cut through?

_____

What is the footnote about?

_____

Look at the chart. What is the black button on the lightsaber called?

_____

# An Origami Lightsaber

Follow the **instructions** to fold four origami lightsabers.

Use the artwork on page 81 as the origami paper.

## HOW TO FOLD A LIGHTSABER

1 | Ask an adult to help you to cut along the dotted lines on page 81. Place the paper for one lightsaber with the arrow pointing up.

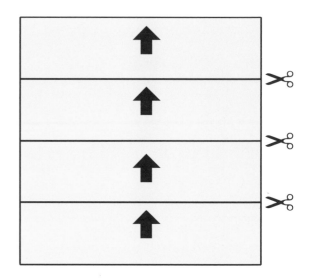

2 Fold just enough to form a thin flap on the left side.

3 Fold in half, lengthwise. Then unfold.

4 Fold the top and the bottom lengthwise to the middle crease. Then unfold.

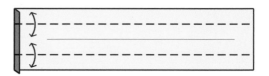

**5** Fold in the bottom-right corner. Then unfold. Turn the paper over.

**6** Fold in the right side.

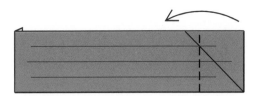

**7** Fold the corners (marked A) into the pockets (marked B). This will turn the model into a triangular tube.

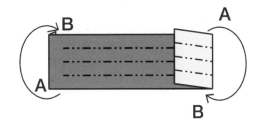

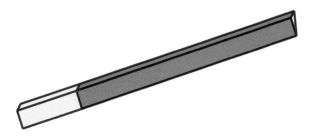

Answer the questions about the origami lightsaber **instructions**.

In Step 3, the instructions tell you to fold and unfold in half "lengthwise". What does "lengthwise" mean?

a) along the long part of the paper

b) diagonally

c) left to right

Which step in the instructions tells you when to turn the paper over?

_____

After following the instructions for step 7, the model

will turn into a _____ tube.

How many lightsabers were you able to fold?

_____

Start with this side facing you.

Start with this side facing you.

Start with this side facing you.

Start with this side facing you.

# Time to Alphabetise

Write all the words in the column on the left in **alphabetical order** on the right.

hermit

sincerely

train

footnote

purple

essay

diagonal

attack

character

detests

quest

_____

_____

_____

_____

_____

_____

_____

_____

_____

_____

Choose any two words and use them in a sentence.

_____

_____

# Galactic History!

The history of the *Star Wars* saga is quite complicated. A **timeline** is a good tool to use to organise events. It can show us how much time has passed between different events and help readers visualise how events fit together.

**41 BBY**

Anakin Skywalker, the Chosen One, who will bring balance to the Force, is born.

**34 BBY**

Anakin Skywalker begins to build C-3PO.

**32 BBY**

Padmé Amidala, former Princess of Theed, is elected Queen of Naboo.

The Trade Federation begins the blockade of Naboo.

Qui-Gon Jinn meets Anakin Skywalker on the planet Tatooine.

The creation of a secret clone army begins on Kamino. Jango Fett, a bounty hunter who wears Mandalorian armour, is the model for the clones.

**22 BBY**

Shmi Skywalker, Anakin's mother, is captured by the Tusken Raiders.

The Clone Wars begin with the Battle of Geonosis.

Anakin Skywalker and Padmé Amidala marry in secret on Naboo.

**19 BBY**

Chancellor Palpatine is revealed to be the Sith Master Darth Sidious.

Anakin Skywalker turns to the dark side of the Force and becomes Darth Vader.

Order 66 is executed: almost all the Jedi are killed.

Luke Skywalker and Leia Organa are born to Padmé Amidala, who dies after they are born.

BBY 41 40 39 38 37 36 35 34 33 32 31 30 29 28 27 26 25 24 23 22 21 20 19 18

**BBY** stands for Before the Battle of Yavin

Read the **timeline**.

Then answer the questions.

## 4 ABY

Han Solo is rescued from Jabba the Hutt.

Yoda dies.

The shield generator is destroyed with the help of the Ewoks in the Battle of Endor.

Darth Vader turns on Palpatine to save Luke's life.

Darth Vader dies after turning back to the light side of the Force.

Without the protection of the shield generator, the Death Star is destroyed by Lando Calrissian, Wedge Antilles and Nien Nunb.

The fall of the Empire and the death of Palpatine are celebrated throughout the galaxy.

## 0 BBY

Princess Leia is captured by Darth Vader.

C-3PO and R2-D2 land on Tatooine where they are found by Luke Skywalker. Luke helps them on their mission to find Obi-Wan Kenobi.

Alderaan is destroyed by the Death Star.

Darth Vader strikes down Obi-Wan Kenobi, allowing Obi-Wan to become one with the Force.

Luke Skywalker destroys the Death Star in the Battle of Yavin.

## 3 ABY

The Battle of Hoth takes place when the Empire discovers the Alliance's secret base on the ice planet.

Luke Skywalker begins his Jedi training with Yoda on the planet Dagobah.

Boba Fett captures Han Solo, who is frozen in carbonite on Cloud City.

Lando Calrissian joins the Rebel Alliance.

Darth Vader reveals to Luke that he is his father.

15  14  13  12  11  10  9  8  7  6  5  4  3  2  1  0  1  2  3  4  ABY

**ABY** stands for After the Battle of Yavin

Answer the questions about the galactic **timeline**.

The timeline begins with what major event?

_____

In 4 ABY, whose life did Darth Vader save?

_____

In what year did the Battle of Hoth take place? _____

In what year was Princess Leia caught by Darth Vader?

_____

Name two events that happened in 22 BBY.

_____

_____

In your opinion, what was the most exciting event that happened before the Battle of Yavin? Why?

_____

_____

What was the most exciting event that happened after the Battle of Yavin?

_____

_____

Draw a picture of your favourite scene from the timeline.

# Start Your Timeline!

On this page, make a list of the most important events in your life, starting with the year you were born. Include things like when you first started to talk and when you started school. List nine events.

_____

_____

_____

_____

_____

_____

_____

_____

# Make Your Own Timeline!

Using the list of important life events you made on page 88, create your own **timeline**.

Write the date, or just the year, and an important event in each box. Then draw a line from each box to the timeline at the bottom.

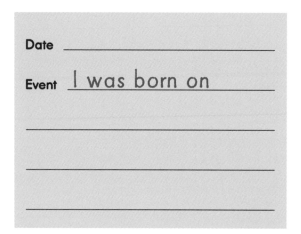

Date _____

Event _I was born on_____

_____

_____

_____

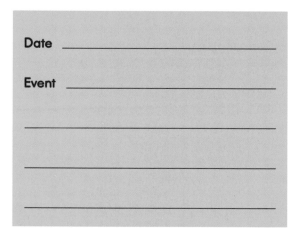

Date _____

Event _____

_____

_____

_____

Date _____

Event _____

_____

_____

_____

_____

Date _____

Event _____

_____

_____

_____

_____

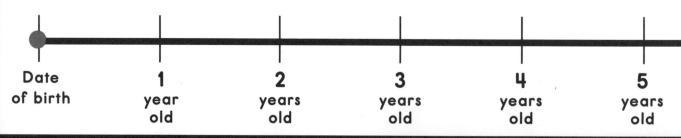

Date of birth    **1** year old    **2** years old    **3** years old    **4** years old    **5** years old

Date _____

Event _____

_____

_____

_____

Date _____

Event _____

_____

_____

_____

Date _____

Event _____

_____

_____

_____

Date _____

Event _____

_____

_____

_____

Date _____

Event _____

_____

_____

_____

_____

Date _____

Event _____

_____

_____

_____

_____

**6**
years
old

**7**
years
old

**8**
years
old

**9**
years
old

**10**
years
old

# Answers

pages 4–5

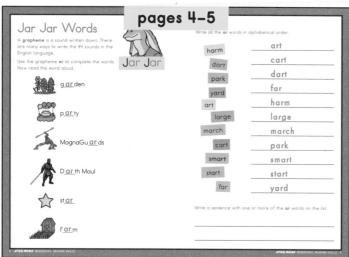

## Jar Jar Words

A **grapheme** is a sound written down. There are many ways to write the 44 sounds in the English language.

Use the grapheme **ar** to complete the words. Now read the word aloud.

g **ar** den

p **ar** ty

MagnaGu **ar** ds

D **ar** th Maul

st **ar**

f **ar** m

Jar Jar

Write all the **ar** words in alphabetical order.

| | |
|---|---|
| harm | art |
| dart | cart |
| park | dart |
| yard | far |
| art | harm |
| large | large |
| march | march |
| cart | park |
| smart | smart |
| start | start |
| far | yard |

Write a sentence with one or more of the **ar** words on the list.

_____

_____

pages 6–7

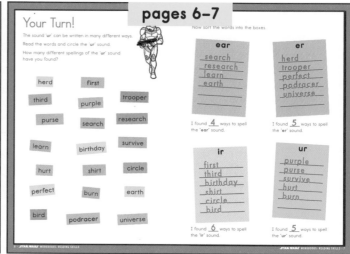

## Your Turn!

The sound 'ur' can be written in many different ways.

Read the words and circle the 'ur' sound.

How many different spellings of the 'ur' sound have you found?

herd  first  trooper

third  purple  research

purse  search  survive

learn  birthday  circle

hurt  shirt  earth

perfect  burn  universe

bird  podracer  universe

Now sort the words into the boxes.

**ear**
search
research
learn
earth

I found **4** ways to spell the '**ear**' sound.

**er**
herd
trooper
perfect
podracer
universe

I found **5** ways to spell the '**er**' sound.

**ir**
first
third
birthday
shirt
circle
bird

I found **6** ways to spell the '**ir**' sound.

**ur**
purple
purse
survive
hurt
burn

I found **5** ways to spell the '**ur**' sound.

pages 8–9

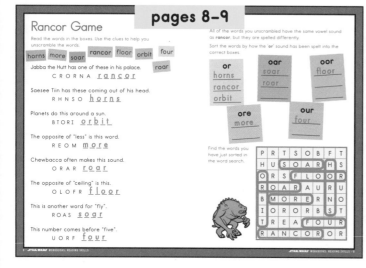

## Rancor Game

Read the words in the boxes. Use the clues to help you unscramble the words.

horns  more  soar  rancor  floor  orbit  four  roar

Jabba the Hutt has one of these in his palace.
C R O R N A **rancor**

Saesee Tiin has these coming out of his head.
R H N S O **horns**

Planets do this around a sun.
B T O R I **orbit**

The opposite of "less" is this word.
R E O M **more**

Chewbacca often makes this sound.
O R A R **roar**

The opposite of "ceiling" is this.
O L O F R **floor**

This is another word for "fly".
R O A S **soar**

This number comes before "five".
U O R F **four**

All of the words you unscrambled have the same vowel sound as **rancor**, but they are spelled differently.

Sort the words by how the 'or' sound has been spelt into the correct boxes.

**or**
horns
rancor
orbit

**oar**
soar
roar

**oor**
floor

**ore**
more

**our**
four

Find the words you have just sorted in the word search.

| P | R | T | S | O | B | F | T |
|---|---|---|---|---|---|---|---|
| H | U | S | O | A | R | H | S |
| O | R | S | F | L | O | O | R |
| R | O | A | R | A | U | R | U |
| B | M | O | R | E | R | N | O |
| I | O | R | O | R | B | S | T |
| T | R | E | A | F | O | U | R |
| R | A | N | C | O | R | O | R |

pages 10–11

## Count Down!

Two common spellings of the 'ow' sound are 'ou' as in **count** and 'ow' as in **down**.

Use 'ow' or 'ou' to complete the words in the crossword grid.

**ACROSS**

3. There are 12 Jedi who sit on the Jedi High (c **ou** ncil).
4. Jar Jar Binks is clumsy. He falls (d **ow** n) a lot!
5. Coruscant is a city full of tall (t **ow** ers).
6. Boba Fett is a (b **ou** nty) hunter.
9. (c **ou** nt) Dooku is also known as Darth Tyranus.
11. Amidala is a queen but she doesn't wear a (cr **ow** n).

**DOWN**

1. The opposite of "whisper" is (sh **ou** t).
2. The Force is a (p **ow** erful) energy field.
6. Wookiees have (br **ow** n) fur.
7. You use a (t **ow** el) to dry yourself.
8. The past tense of "find" is (f **ou** nd).
10. Mos Espa is a (t **ow** n) on Tatooine.

Crossword grid:
- council
- down
- towers
- bounty
- crown
- shout
- powerful
- brown
- towel
- found
- count
- town

pages 12–13

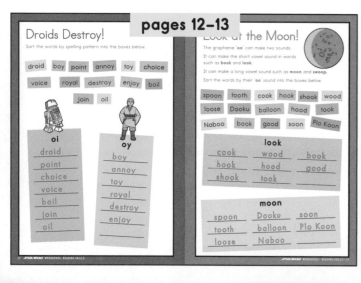

## Droids Destroy!

Sort the words by spelling pattern into the boxes below.

droid  boy  point  annoy  toy  choice  voice  royal  destroy  enjoy  boil  join  oil

**oi**
droid
point
choice
voice
boil
join
oil

**oy**
boy
annoy
toy
royal
destroy
enjoy

## Look at the Moon!

The grapheme 'oo' can make two sounds.

It can make the short vowel sound in words such as **book** and **look**.

It can make a long vowel sound such as **moon** and **swoop**.

Sort the words by their 'oo' sound into the boxes below.

spoon  tooth  cook  hook  shook  wood  loose  Dooku  balloon  hood  took  Naboo  book  good  soon  Plo Koon

**look**
cook  wood  book
hook  hood  good
shook  took

**moon**
spoon  Dooku  soon
tooth  balloon  Plo Koon
loose  Naboo

pages 14–15

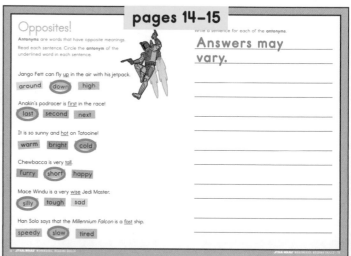

## Opposites!

**Antonyms** are words that have opposite meanings.

Read each sentence. Circle the **antonym** of the underlined word in each sentence.

Jango Fett can fly <u>up</u> in the air with his jetpack.
around  (down)  high

Anakin's podracer is <u>first</u> in the race!
(last)  second  next

It is so sunny and <u>hot</u> on Tatooine!
warm  bright  (cold)

Chewbacca is very <u>tall</u>.
furry  (short)  happy

Mace Windu is a very <u>wise</u> Jedi Master.
(silly)  tough  sad

Han Solo says that the *Millennium Falcon* is a <u>fast</u> ship.
speedy  (slow)  tired

Write a sentence for each of the **antonyms**.

**Answers may vary.**

_____

_____

_____

_____

_____

_____

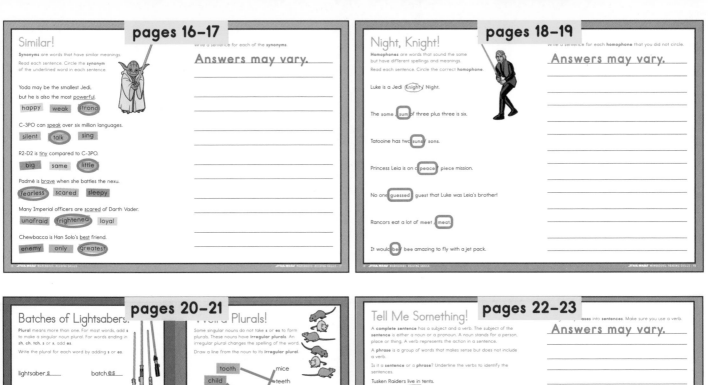

**pages 16–17**

## Similar!

**Synonyms** are words that have similar meanings.
Read each sentence. Circle the **synonym** of the underlined word in each sentence.

Yoda may be the smallest Jedi, but he is also the most <u>powerful</u>.
happy   weak   (strong)

C-3PO can <u>speak</u> over six million languages.
silent   (talk)   sing

R2-D2 is <u>tiny</u> compared to C-3PO.
big   same   (little)

Padmé is <u>brave</u> when she battles the nexu.
(fearless)   scared   sleepy

Many Imperial officers are <u>scared</u> of Darth Vader.
unafraid   (frightened)   loyal

Chewbacca is Han Solo's <u>best</u> friend.
enemy   only   (greatest)

write a sentence for each of the **synonyms**.
**Answers may vary.**

**pages 18–19**

## Night, Knight!

**Homophones** are words that sound the same but have different spellings and meanings.
Read each sentence. Circle the correct **homophone**.

Luke is a Jedi (Knight)/ Night.

The some /(sum)of three plus three is six.

Tatooine has two(suns)/ sons.

Princess Leia is on a(peace)/ piece mission.

No one (guessed)/ guest that Luke was Leia's brother!

Rancors eat a lot of meet /(meat.)

It would be(be)/ bee amazing to fly with a jet pack.

write a sentence for each **homophone** that you did not circle.
**Answers may vary.**

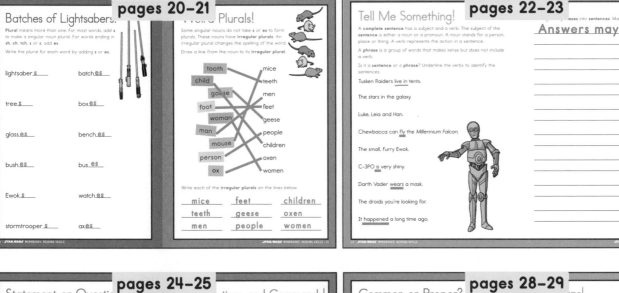

**pages 20–21**

## Batches of Lightsabers!

**Plural** means more than one. For most words, add **s** to make a singular noun plural. For words ending in **sh, ch, tch, s** or **x**, add **es**.

Write the plural for each word by adding **s** or **es**.

lightsaber**s**      batch**es**

tree**s**      box**es**

glass**es**      bench**es**

bush**es**      bus.**es**

Ewok**s**      watch**es**

stormtrooper**s**      ax**es**

## Weird Plurals!

Some singular nouns do not take **s** or **es** to form plurals. These nouns have **irregular plurals**. An irregular plural changes the spelling of the word.

Draw a line from the noun to its **irregular plural**.

tooth — teeth
child — children
goose — geese
foot — feet
woman — women
man — men
mouse — mice
person — people
ox — oxen

Write each of the **irregular plurals** on the lines below.

| mice | feet | children |
|------|------|----------|
| teeth | geese | oxen |
| men | people | women |

**pages 22–23**

## Tell Me Something!

A **complete sentence** has a subject and a verb. The subject of the **sentence** is either a noun or a pronoun. A noun stands for a person, place or thing. A verb represents the action in a sentence.

A **phrase** is a group of words that makes sense but does not include a verb.

Is it a **sentence** or a **phrase**? Underline the verbs to identify the sentences.

Tusken Raiders <u>live</u> in tents.

The stars in the galaxy.

Luke, Leia and Han.

Chewbacca can <u>fly</u> the *Millennium Falcon*.

The small, furry Ewok.

C-3PO <u>is</u> very shiny.

Darth Vader <u>wears</u> a mask.

The droids you're looking for.

It <u>happened</u> a long time ago.

write phrases into sentences. Make sure you use a verb.
**Answers may vary.**

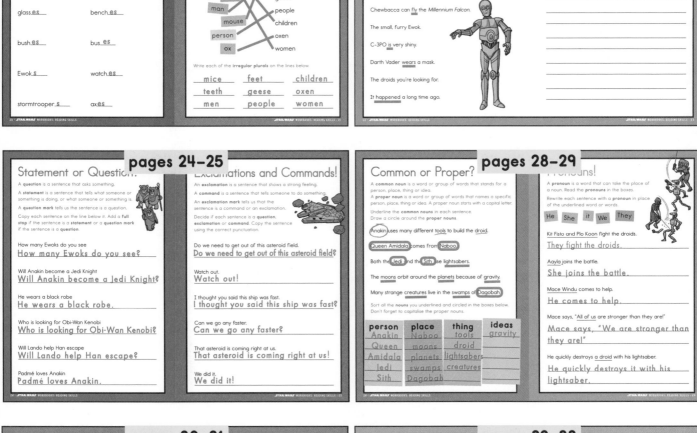

**pages 24–25**

## Statement or Question?

A **question** is a sentence that asks something.
A **statement** is a sentence that tells what someone or something is doing, or what someone or something is.
A **question mark** tells us the sentence is a question.
Copy each sentence on the line below it. Add a **full stop** if the sentence is a **statement** or a **question mark** if the sentence is a **question**.

How many Ewoks do you see
**How many Ewoks do you see?**

Will Anakin become a Jedi Knight
**Will Anakin become a Jedi Knight?**

He wears a black robe
**He wears a black robe.**

Who is looking for Obi-Wan Kenobi
**Who is looking for Obi-Wan Kenobi?**

Will Lando help Han escape
**Will Lando help Han escape?**

Padmé loves Anakin
**Padmé loves Anakin.**

## Exclamations and Commands!

An **exclamation** is a sentence that shows a strong feeling.
A **command** is a sentence that tells someone to do something.
An **exclamation mark** tells us that the sentence is a command or an exclamation.
Decide if each sentence is a **question**, **exclamation** or **command**. Copy the sentence using the correct punctuation.

Do we need to get out of this asteroid field.
**Do we need to get out of this asteroid field?**

Watch out.
**Watch out!**

I thought you said this ship was fast.
**I thought you said this ship was fast?**

Can we go any faster.
**Can we go any faster?**

That asteroid is coming right at us.
**That asteroid is coming right at us!**

We did it.
**We did it!**

**pages 28–29**

## Common or Proper?

A **common noun** is a word or group of words that stands for a person, place, thing or idea.
A **proper noun** is a word or group of words that names a specific person, place, thing or idea. A proper noun starts with a capital letter.
Underline the **common nouns** in each sentence.
Draw a circle around the **proper nouns**.

(Anakin) uses many different <u>tools</u> to build the <u>droid</u>.

(Queen Amidala) comes from (Naboo.)

Both the <u>Jedi</u> and the (Sith) use <u>lightsabers</u>.

The <u>moons</u> orbit around the <u>planets</u> because of <u>gravity</u>.

Many strange <u>creatures</u> live in the <u>swamps</u> of (Dagobah)

Sort all the **nouns** you underlined and circled in the boxes below. Don't forget to capitalise the proper nouns.

| person | place | thing | ideas |
|--------|-------|-------|-------|
| Anakin | Naboo | tools | gravity |
| Queen | moons | droid | |
| Amidala | planets | lightsabers | |
| Jedi | swamps | creatures | |
| Sith | Dagobah | | |

## Pronouns!

A **pronoun** is a word that can take the place of a noun. Read the **pronouns** in the boxes.
Rewrite each sentence with a **pronoun** in place of the underlined word or words.

He   She   It   We   They

Kit Fisto and Plo Koon fight the droids.
**They fight the droids.**

Aayla joins the battle.
**She joins the battle.**

Mace Windu comes to help.
**He comes to help.**

Mace says, "All of us are stronger than they are!"
**Mace says, "We are stronger than they are!"**

He quickly destroys a droid with his lightsaber.
**He quickly destroys it with his lightsaber.**

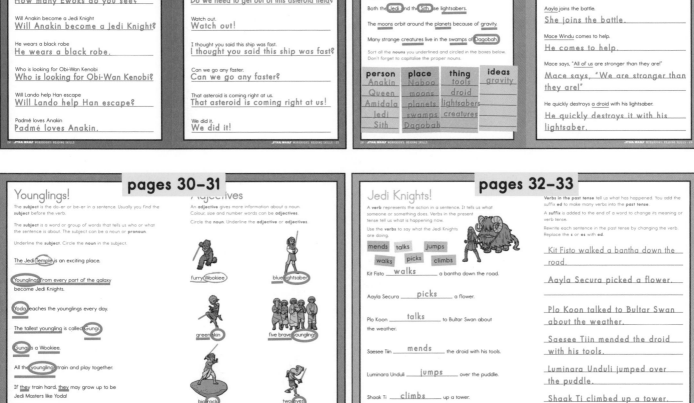

**pages 30–31**

## Younglings!

The **subject** is the do-er or be-er in a sentence. Usually you find the **subject** before the verb.

The **subject** is a word or group of words that tells us who or what the sentence is about. The subject can be a noun or **pronoun**.

Underline the **subject**. Circle the **noun** in the subject.

<u>The Jedi (temple)</u> is an exciting place.

<u>(Younglings) from every part of the galaxy</u> become Jedi Knights.

<u>(Yoda)</u> teaches the younglings every day.

<u>The tallest youngling is called (Gungi)</u>.

<u>(Gungi)</u> is a Wookiee.

All the <u>younglings</u> train and play together.

If <u>(they)</u> train hard, <u>(they)</u> may grow up to be Jedi Masters like Yoda!

## Adjectives

An **adjective** gives more information about a noun. Colour, size and number words can be **adjectives**.
Circle the **noun**. Underline the **adjective** or **adjectives**.

<u>furry</u> (Wookiee)

<u>blue</u> (lightsaber)

<u>green</u> (skin)

<u>five brave</u> (younglings)

<u>big</u> (rock)

<u>two</u> (eyes)

**pages 32–33**

## Jedi Knights!

A **verb** represents the action in a sentence. It tells us what someone or something does. Verbs in the present tense tell us what is happening now.
Use the **verbs** to say what the Jedi Knights are doing.

mends   talks   jumps
walks   picks   climbs

Kit Fisto **walks** a bantha down the road.

Aayla Secura **picks** a flower.

Plo Koon **talks** to Bultar Swan about the weather.

Saesee Tiin **mends** the droid with his tools.

Luminara Unduli **jumps** over the puddle.

Shaak Ti **climbs** up a tower.

**Verbs** in the **past tense** tell us what has happened. You add the suffix **ed** to make many verbs into the **past tense**.
A **suffix** is added to the end of a word to change its meaning or verb tense.
Rewrite each sentence in the past tense by changing the verb. Replace the **s** or **es** with **ed**.

**Kit Fisto walked a bantha down the road.**

**Aayla Secura picked a flower.**

**Plo Koon talked to Bultar Swan about the weather.**

**Saesee Tiin mended the droid with his tools.**

**Luminara Unduli jumped over the puddle.**

**Shaak Ti climbed up a tower.**

# Answers

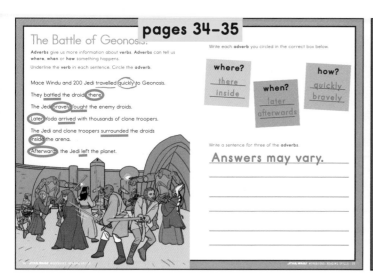

**The Battle of Geonosis**

**Adverbs** give us more information about **verbs**. Adverbs can tell us **where**, **when** or **how** something happens.

Underline the **verb** in each sentence. Circle the **adverb**.

Mace Windu and 200 Jedi travelled (quickly) to Geonosis.

They battled the droids (there).

The Jedi (bravely) fought the enemy droids.

(Later,) Yoda arrived with thousands of clone troopers.

The Jedi and clone troopers surrounded the droids (inside) the arena.

(Afterwards,) the Jedi left the planet.

Write each **adverb** you circled in the correct box below.

**where?**
_there_
_inside_

**when?**
_later_
_afterwards_

**how?**
_quickly_
_bravely_

Write a sentence for three of the **adverbs**.

_Answers may vary._

---

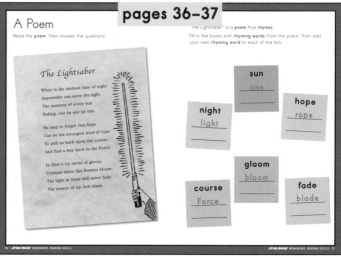

**A Poem**

Read the **poem**. Then answer the questions.

### The Lightsaber

When in the darkest time of night
Impossible can seem the light,
The memory of every sun
Fading, one by one by one.

So easy to forget that hope
Can be the strongest kind of rope
To pull us back upon the course;
And find a way back to the Force.

In Ilum's icy caves of gloom,
Crystals shine like flowers bloom,
The light in them will never fade:
The source of my Jedi blade.

"The Lightsaber" is a **poem** that rhymes.

Fill in the boxes with **rhyming words** from the poem. Then add your own **rhyming word** to each of the lists.

**sun**
_one_

**night**
_light_

**hope**
_rope_

**gloom**
_bloom_

**course**
_Force_

**fade**
_blade_

---

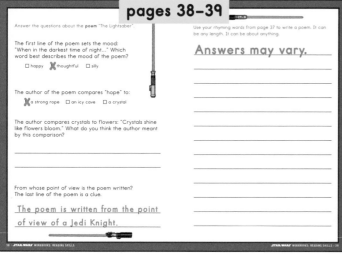

Answer the questions about the **poem** "The Lightsaber".

The first line of the poem sets the mood:
"When in the darkest time of night..." Which word best describes the mood of the poem?

☐ happy ☒ thoughtful ☐ silly

The author of the poem compares "hope" to:

☒ a strong rope ☐ an icy cave ☐ a crystal

The author compares crystals to flowers: "Crystals shine like flowers bloom." What do you think the author meant by this comparison?

_____

From whose point of view is the poem written? The last line of the poem is a clue.

_The poem is written from the point_
_of view of a Jedi Knight._

Use your rhyming words from page 37 to write a poem. It can be any length. It can be about anything.

_Answers may vary._

---

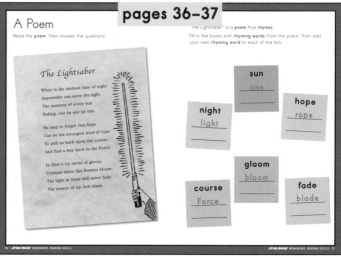

**A Fable**

Read the **fable**. Answer the questions about each part of the story.

### The Ewoks and the Duloks

Once upon a time on the forest moon of Endor, a big storm began to brew in the mountains.

The Ewoks, seeing the dark clouds above the mountains, prepared for the storm. They threw ropes around the oldest trees to brace them against the wind. They dug shelters underground, which they covered with wax to make them waterproof. They gathered as many nuts and berries as they could find, and stored them away inside the shelters.

The Duloks, seeing their cousins toiling so hard, were scornful.

"Why are you all working so much?" they asked.

"There is a big storm brewing in the mountains!" answered the Ewoks. "The storm is heading towards us. We are making sure we have enough to eat in case the storm lasts a long time."

• 1 •

The Duloks looked up. The sky was clear and blue, and the sun shone brightly. The passing breeze was gentle. The air smelled of almonds and lavender.

"What storm?" the Duloks replied scornfully. "It is a beautiful day! And there is plenty to eat! Why worry about storms that may come tomorrow when today is so bright and lovely?"

The Ewoks shrugged and kept on working.

The Duloks laughed.

"What silly Ewoks you are!" they said, and went off to play.

• 2 •

Where is the story set?

_The story is set on the forest moon_
_of Endor._

How would you describe the Ewoks?
(Tick as many boxes as you want)

☒ hardworking ☐ rude ☐ nice
☒ clever ☐ lazy ☐ mean

How would you describe the Duloks?
(Tick as many boxes as you want)

☐ hardworking ☒ rude ☐ nice
☐ clever ☒ lazy ☒ mean

---

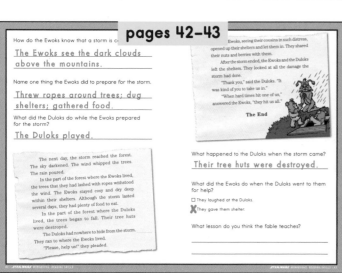

How do the Ewoks know that a storm is coming?

_The Ewoks see the dark clouds_
_above the mountains._

Name one thing the Ewoks did to prepare for the storm.

_Threw ropes around trees; dug_
_shelters; gathered food._

What did the Duloks do while the Ewoks prepared for the storm?

_The Duloks played._

The next day, the storm reached the forest. The sky darkened. The wind whipped the trees. The rain poured.

In the part of the forest where the Ewoks lived, the trees that they had lashed with ropes withstood the wind. The Ewoks stayed cosy and dry deep within their shelters. Although the storm lasted several days, they had plenty of food to eat.

In the part of the forest where the Duloks lived, the trees began to fall. Their tree huts were destroyed.

The Duloks had nowhere to hide from the storm. They ran to where the Ewoks lived.

"Please, help us!" they pleaded.

The Ewoks, seeing their cousins in such distress, opened up their shelters and let them in. They shared their nuts and berries with them.

After the storm ended, the Ewoks and the Duloks left the shelters. They looked at all the damage the storm had done.

"Thank you," said the Duloks. "It was kind of you to take us in."

"When hard times hit one of us," answered the Ewoks, "they hit us all."

**The End**

What happened to the Duloks when the storm came?

_Their tree huts were destroyed._

What did the Ewoks do when the Duloks went to them for help?

☐ They laughed at the Duloks.
☒ They gave them shelter.

What lesson do you think the fable teaches?

_____

---

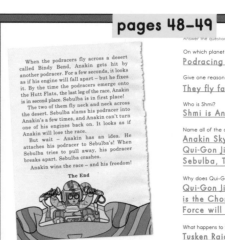

When the podracers fly across a desert called Bindy Bend, Anakin gets hit by another podracer. For a few seconds, it looks as if his engine will fall apart – but he fixes it. By the time the podracers emerge onto the Hutt Flats, the last leg of the race, Anakin is in second place. Sebulba is in first place!

The two of them fly neck and neck across the desert. Sebulba slams his podracer into Anakin's a few times, and Anakin can't turn one of his engines back on. It looks as if Anakin will lose the race.

But wait – Anakin has an idea. He attaches his podracer to Sebulba's! When Sebulba tries to pull away, his podracer breaks apart. Sebulba crashes.

Anakin wins the race – and his freedom!

**The End**

Answer the questions about the **action story** "The Podrace".

On which planet is podracing a very popular sport?

_Podracing is popular on Tatooine._

Give one reason why podracing is a dangerous sport.

_They fly fast. They crash._

Who is Shmi?

_Shmi is Anakin's mother._

Name all of the characters in the story.

_Anakin Skywalker, Shmi, Watto,_
_Qui-Gon Jinn, Padmé Amidala,_
_Sebulba, Tusken Raiders._

Why does Qui-Gon Jinn think that Anakin will win?

_Qui-Gon Jinn believes that Anakin_
_is the Chosen One and that the_
_Force will help him win._

What happens to the podracers in the Canyon Dune Turn?

_Tusken Raiders fire blasters at them._

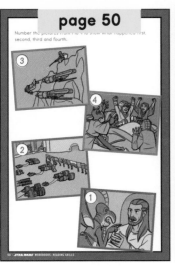

Number the pictures from 1 to 4 to show what happened first, second, third and fourth.

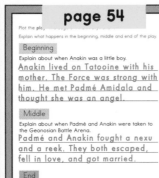

Plot the play... ...

Explain what happens in the beginning, middle and end of the play.

**Beginning**

Explain about when Anakin was a little boy.

Anakin lived on Tatooine with his mother. The Force was strong with him. He met Padmé Amidala and thought she was an angel.

**Middle**

Explain about when Padmé and Anakin were taken to the Geonosian Battle Arena.

Padmé and Anakin fought a nexu and a reek. They both escaped, fell in love, and got married.

**End**

Explain about when Anakin turned to the dark side of the Force.

Anakin lost a lightsaber duel with Obi-Wan Kenobi. Anakin was rescued by Darth Sidious on Mustafar. Darth Sidious turned Anakin into his apprentice, Darth Vader.

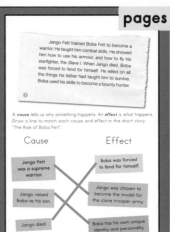
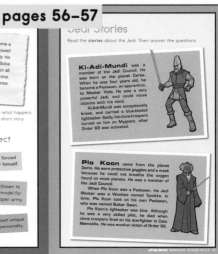

**Jedi Stories**

Read the **stories** about the Jedi. Then answer the questions.

Jango Fett trained Boba Fett to become a warrior. He taught him combat skills. He showed him how to use his armour, and how to fly his starfighter, the *Slave I*. When Jango died, Boba was forced to fend for himself. Boba relied on all the things his father had taught him to survive. Boba used his skills to become a bounty hunter.

**Ki-Adi-Mundi** was a member of the Jedi Council. He was born on the planet Cerea. When he was four years old, he became a Padawan, an apprentice, to Master Yoda. He was a very powerful Jedi, and could move objects with his mind. Ki-Adi-Mundi was exceptionally brave, and carried a blue-bladed lightsaber. Sadly, his clone troopers turned on him on Mygeeto, after Order 66 was activated.

**Plo Koon** came from the planet Dorin. He wore protective goggles and a mask because he could not breathe the oxygen found on most planets. He was a member of the Jedi Council. When Plo Koon was a Padawan, his Jedi Master was a Wookiee named Tyvokka. In time, Plo Koon took on his own Padawan, who was named Bultar Swan. Plo Koon's lightsaber was blue. Although he was a very skilled pilot, he died when clone troopers fired on his starfighter in Cato Neimoidia. He was another victim of Order 66.

A **cause** tells us why something happens. An **effect** is what happens. Draw a line to match each cause and effect in the short story "The Rise of Boba Fett".

**Cause** — **Effect**

Jango Fett was a supreme warrior. → Jango was chosen to become the model for the clone trooper army.

Jango raised Boba as his son. → Boba has his own unique identity and personality.

Jango died. → Boba was forced to fend for himself.

Who is who? Write the name of the character on... next to each picture.

Plo Koon

Ki-Adi-Mundi

Aayla Secura

Shaak Ti

Kit Fisto

...y details in each story. Answer the questions about the Jedi stories.

Which Jedi did not have a blue lightsaber?

Kit Fisto did not have a blue lightsaber.

When Ki-Adi-Mundi was a Padawan, who was his Jedi Master?

Yoda was Ki-Adi-Mundi's Jedi Master.

Who was responsible for issuing Order 66?

Supreme Chancellor Palpatine issued Order 66.

Which Jedi was a Twi'lek?

Aayla Secura was a Twi'lek.

Circle the part of Kit Fisto's body that helps him be a good swimmer.

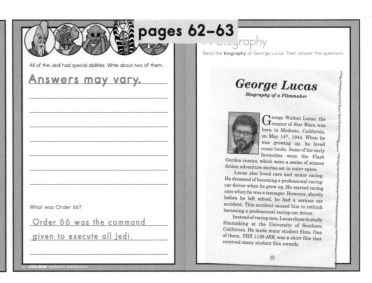

All of the Jedi had special abilities. Write about two of them.

Answers may vary.

What was Order 66?

Order 66 was the command given to execute all Jedi.

**A Biography**

Read the **biography** of George Lucas. Then answer the questions.

**George Lucas**
*Biography of a Filmmaker*

George Walton Lucas, the creator of *Star Wars*, was born in Modesto, California, on May 14th, 1944. When he was growing up, he loved comic books. Some of his early favourites were the Flash Gordon comics, which were a series of science fiction adventure stories set in outer space.

Lucas also loved cars and motor racing. He dreamed of becoming a professional racing-car driver when he grew up. He started racing cars when he was a teenager. However, shortly before he left school, he had a serious car accident. This accident caused him to rethink becoming a professional racing-car driver.

Instead of racing cars, Lucas chose to study filmmaking at the University of Southern California. He made many student films. One of them, *THX 1138 4EB*, was a short film that received many student film awards.

Answer the questions about the biography of Ge... Circle the correct answers.

What is the main subject of the biography?
a) The creation of Lucasfilm.
b) Where George Lucas was born.
c) Racing-car driving.
d) How George Lucas became a filmmaker and made *Star Wars*.

Based on the biography, why did George Lucas decide to study filmmaking?
a) He went to the University of Southern California.
b) A racing-car accident made him decide not to become a racing-car driver.
c) He had always loved films.
d) He founded Lucasfilm.

What was the name of the film that came out in 1977?
a) *American Graffiti*
b) *Star Wars*
c) *THX 1138 4EB*
d) *Flash Gordon*

What happened when *Star Wars* came out?
a) It became the most popular film of all time.
b) George Lucas decided to retire.
c) George Lucas created *American Graffiti*.
d) George Lucas founded Lucasfilm.

...word to complete each sentence.

George Lucas _____ cars and motor racing.
disliked / **loved** / liked

*American Graffiti* was _____ by George Lucas's high-school experience.
made / loved / **inspired**

George Lucas wanted to make an _____ story set in outer space.
exciting / **adventure** / upsetting

After *Star Wars* came out, Darth Vader became a _____ character to people around the world.
**familiar** / hated / beloved

Based on the text, why is it a good thing that George Lucas did not become a racing-car driver?

If he had become a racing car driver, the world might never have had 'Star Wars'.

CINEMA — STAR WARS

**A Letter to George Lucas**

Here is a fan letter to George Lucas. The parts of the letter have been labelled, but there are some grammatical mistakes. Use the proofreading marks below to edit the mistakes.

Add text — Add a full stop — Add a question mark
Capitalize letter — Take out — Spelling error

Mr George Lucas      Heading
Lucasfilm
1110 Gorgas Avenue
San Francisco, CA 94129

Dear Mr Lucas,      Greeting

I love your movies! I like all six of them, but my favourite is Attack of the Clones. It was cool how Padmé, Obi-Wan and Anakin for the arena creatures. I also liked how the clone tropers helped the Jedi. There is one mistake.

I heard you are making three new movies. Will those be about Luke Skywalker? I can't wait to see them.

Yours Sincerely,      Closing

Cary (age 10)      Signature

**A Letter From You**

Would you like to write a letter to George Lucas? Write a first draft of it here.

Answers may vary.

Now proofread your letter to make sure you haven't made any mistakes. Use this checklist to make sure!

☐ Are all the words spelled correctly?
☐ Does every sentence begin with a capital letter?
☐ Does every sentence end with a full stop or a question mark?
☐ Are names capitalised?
☐ Do you have a heading, greeting, body, closing and signature?

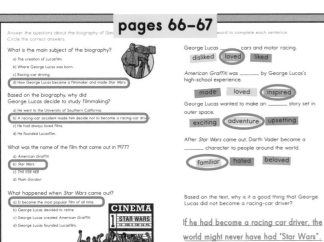

The sentences below are all highlighted in the article.

Put a cross by the meaning that fits the underlined word in each sentence.

Luke <u>craves</u> adventure.
☒ wants   ☐ hates

The droids lead Luke to Obi-Wan Kenobi, a <u>wise</u> old hermit living in the desert.
☒ thoughtful   ☐ friend

Vader was once a <u>pupil</u> of Obi-Wan Kenobi, who had trained him to become a Jedi Knight.
☐ teacher   ☒ student

Now Vader uses his force powers for evil <u>on behalf of</u> the Empire.
☐ on half of   ☒ on the side of

Will the Rebel Alliance <u>defeat</u> the Empire?
☒ beat   ☐ lose to

Draw a line from the vocabulary words used in the article (in the blue boxes) to the words that mean the same thing (in the yellow boxes).

plot — storyline
remote — distant, hard to get to
quest — a search for, hunt
evil — bad
thrilling — exciting, fun

Write a sentence for each of the words.

Answers may vary.

**All About Lightsabers**

Read the **essay** about lightsabers. Then answer the questions.

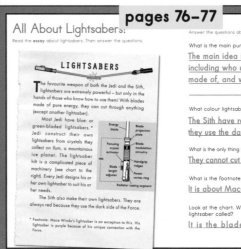

**LIGHTSABERS**

The favourite weapon of both the Jedi and the Sith, lightsabers are extremely powerful – but only in the hands of those who know how to use them! With blades made of pure energy, they can cut through anything (except another lightsaber).

Most Jedi have blue- or green-bladed lightsabers. Jedi construct their own lightsabers from crystals they collect on Ilum, a mountainous ice planet. The lightsaber hilt is a complicated piece of machinery (see chart to the right). Every Jedi designs his or her own lightsaber to suit his or her needs.

The Sith also make their own lightsabers. They are always red because they use the dark side of the Force.

* Footnote: Mace Windu's lightsaber is an exception to this. His lightsaber is purple because of his unique connection with the Force.

Energy blade — Blade projection plate — Focusing crystal activator — Blade emitter — Blade modulation circuitry — Handgrip ridges — Blade length adjuster — Power vortex ring — Radiator casing tensioner

Answer the questions about the essay on lightsabers.

What is the main purpose of this essay?

The main idea is to tell about lightsabers, including who uses them, what they are made of, and what the colours mean.

What colour lightsabers do the Sith have? Why?

The Sith have red lightsabers because they use the dark side of the Force.

What is the only thing that lightsabers cannot cut through?

They cannot cut through other lightsabers.

What is the footnote about?

It is about Mace Windu's lightsaber.

Look at the chart. What is the black button on the lightsaber called?

It is the blade length adjuster.

# Answers

## pages 80-81

Answer the questions about the origami lightsaber instructions.

In Step 3, the instructions tell you to fold and unfold in half "lengthwise". What does "lengthwise" mean?

(a) along the long part of the paper

b) diagonally

c) left to right

Which step in the instructions tells you when to turn the paper over?

Step 5 tells when to turn the paper over.

After following the instructions for step 7, the model will turn into a _____triangular_____ tube.

How many lightsabers were you able to fold?

_____

## pages 82-83

Time to Alphabetise

Write all the words in the column on the left in **alphabetical order** on the right.

| | |
|---|---|
| hermit | attack |
| sincerely | character |
| train | detests |
| footnote | diagonal |
| purple | essay |
| essay | footnote |
| diagonal | hermit |
| attack | purple |
| character | quest |
| detests | sincerely |
| quest | train |

Choose any two words and use them in a sentence.

Answers may vary.

_____

## pages 86-87

Answer the questions about the galactic timeline.

The timeline begins with what major event?
Anakin Skywalker is born.

In 4 ABY, whose life did Darth Vader save?
Darth Vader saves Luke Skywalker's life.

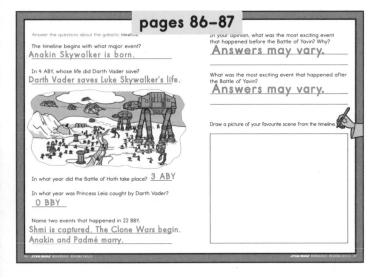

In what year did the Battle of Hoth take place? 3 ABY

In what year was Princess Leia caught by Darth Vader?
0 BBY

Name two events that happened in 22 BBY.
Shmi is captured. The Clone Wars begin.
Anakin and Padmé marry.

In your opinion, what was the most exciting event that happened before the Battle of Yavin? Why?
Answers may vary.

What was the most exciting event that happened after the Battle of Yavin?
Answers may vary.

_____

Draw a picture of your favourite scene from the timeline.